NEVER WEAR WHITE TO A JUNGLE JUICE PARTY

NEVER WEAR WHITE TO A JUNGLE JUICE PARTY

and Other Legit College Tips and Hacks

Stattin Yates
Illustrated by Michele Smith

DREAM. THINK. BE., LLC

Omaha, Nebraska

NEVER WEAR WHITE TO A JUNGLE JUICE PARTY
AND OTHER LEGIT COLLEGE TIPS AND HACKS

© 2016 Text Stattin Yates
© 2016 Illustrations Michele Smith

Publishing and publicity inquiries can be sent to:

Dream. Think. Be., LLC
c/o Concierge Marketing Inc.
13518 L. Street
Omaha, NE 68137
402-884-5995

www.JungleJuiceParty.com

ISBN: 978-0-9973945-1-1 (ppk)
ISBN: 978-0-9973945-2-8 (mobi)
ISBN: 978-0-9973945-3-5 (epub)

LCCN: 2016935887
Library of Congress CIP Data on file with the Publisher

Printed in the USA

10 9 8 7 6 5 4 3 2 1

This book is for my family, my friends, my teachers, my students, and even my foes. Without them, none of these stories would have taken place. You are the people who made college worthwhile and this book possible. I've listened to all your advice—some great, some horrendous—but in the end, I've learned from it all, and for that, I am forever grateful. It was through our experiences together that I learned to dream big, think clearly, and be endless. Cheers to health and happiness. May our hearts be light and our drinks be strong.

CONTENTS

ACADEMIA

*Classes, presentations,
and mental preparation.*

No matter how much you study or how prepared you think you are, there will always be things you could have done differently. Don't focus on that. The important part of classwork is that you learn the intended message and use it to infer other ideas. As long as your grades are good enough to earn credits and continue on towards your degree, don't worry about the numbers. Just work hard and never second-guess yourself.

1. Don't unwrap textbooks until you need them.

Most bookstores have strict return policies. Don't break the seal until needed, and if you haven't used a book in the first two weeks of class, return it; you can always buy it again.

I learned this the hard way during my sophomore year. I was angry after finding out that the only difference between the new version and the older version of my textbook was that the author had added a glossary. I had already opened the new version, which cost me $79. I tried returning it, but the bookstore manager wouldn't allow me to because it had been opened, which meant they had no way of knowing if the website password included in the purchase had already been activated. Despite me promising it hadn't, they refused my return. I then decided I'd just eat the difference of the price and sell it back as a used book. However, they told me they couldn't buy back used books at that time. After searching high and low, I was finally able to find a bookstore that bought it back from me as a used book... for one dollar. The takeaway? Consider not buying a textbook until you actually need it.

2. Make at least one friend in every class.

You'll need a co-conspirator that one time you "forget to sign the attendance sheet."

3. Make friends with a teacher's aide.

They're a living answer key.

4. Dress nicely on test days.

Studies show you're more likely to pass the test if you're dressed seriously. If you don't pass the test, at least you're already dressed for your own funeral.

5. Register for classes as soon as possible.

Classes are one of the few things in the world that are still first come, first serve. Don't blow it!

6. Try to buy used books and/or buy books online.

It seems too easy these days, but make sure you look high and low before you pay retail prices for your books.

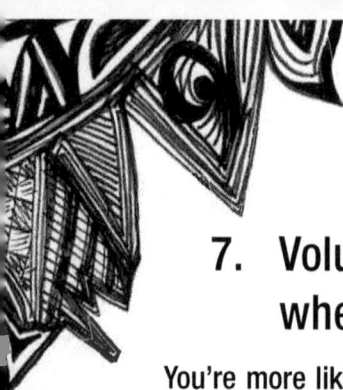

7. Volunteer to present first when giving speeches.

You're more likely to get a good grade if you're the one setting the standard.

Presenting first is a great move. It gives you a chance to show you have confidence in your work and to set the tone for the whole class; just make sure you're also physically ready. I remember jumping at the chance to present first on a speech I had written about Malcolm X. After I got to the podium, I realized I still had a piece of gum in my mouth. This professor was a stickler for status-quo, and I knew the gum in my mouth would've been a major strike against me. I tucked the gum into my cheek with my tongue and starting speaking. As I was talking, she would look down at her book to take notes about my speech. The gum was starting to irritate me, and I felt like she was about to notice. When she glanced back down at her book to write a note, I looked straight down towards my feet, opened my mouth, and let the gum fall out, all while continuing with my speech. The class erupted with laughter, and she quickly looked up with a suspicious look on her face. Despite this, I kept on with my presentation without a glitch and ended up with an A. The takeaway? If you're going to present first, make sure you show up—both mentally and physically.

8. Put a cover sheet on everything you submit.

Appearance is 9/10 of the law. Something that looks serious will be taken seriously.

9. Back up all important documents on more than one flash drive.

The reason the flash drive was free is because they come a dime a dozen these days, but with that comes a less dependable product. If the work you did was important enough to save, consider saving it to a backup.

10. Refer to your instructor as professor, not teacher.

This isn't high school anymore.

11. Proofread every paper.

Spell check is by no means foolproof. The computer won't recognize a misspelling when the job application you turn in says "pubic relations specialist."

12. Try studying in places other than the library.

Research shows studying in an environment and mindset similar to your test environment will increase your ability to recall information.

13. Email yourself all of your papers and reports.

Not only is this a near foolproof way of having access to your important documents, but it also gives you a time stamp to find your most updated version.

14. Ask your professors what style they prefer for bibliographies and source citing.

Check your syllabus before asking so you don't look like a clown.

15. Listen to everything other students say in class.

Even if it's the kid who just talks to sound smart, tune in. More importantly, listen to the professor's response to avoid missing out on crucial information.

16. Go to class.

All professors take note of who shows up regularly. Even if they don't appear to be marking it in a book, mentally they take note. But don't go if you're actually contagious.

My junior year, I took a remedial math class to get my one math credit. My professor was probably a year away from retirement and never took attendance. I couldn't have cared less about this class, and apparently, it was painfully obvious to the professor. She hated me. This was a math class I had already taken in my freshman year of high school so it was very easy. I rarely showed up. Eventually, my lack of caring caught up to me, and I fell to a C in the class. When it came time for the final, I studied hard to make sure I wouldn't fall from that C, as a D will get you a credit, but doesn't count towards your degree. I did awesome. I got a B on the final. I knew, coupled with my C average in the class, I was golden. Grades were posted a week later, and much to my disappointment, I was "awarded" a D. I disputed this with the college, who told me I got that grade because of poor attendance, and they backed the professor's decision. I had to redo this class, even though I never saw her take attendance once. The takeaway? Just go to class.

17. Have separate notebooks for every class.

Okay, okay, maybe not spiral notebooks, but make sure your computer or tablet is organized.

18. Ask upperclassmen which professors they recommend.

Don't you want to know who takes attendance and who doesn't?

19. Make sure your name is spelled correctly on the class roster.

Otherwise, Sara could get the credit for an exam instead of Sarah, and in a worst-case scenario, credit for the whole class.

20. Don't spend too much time getting ready for an early class.

It's early—nobody cares.

21. Be on time to class and show enthusiasm.

Appearing to care could be the difference between a D and an F.

22. Always cite your sources.

Although, a wise man once said, "You're a nobody until you've been sued."

23. Don't eat loud snacks in class.

Being annoying is the quickest way to make enemies.

24. It's better to stay up late to finish an assignment than it is to try to wake up early to do it.

Let's put it this way—it's easier to turn in an assignment tired than it is to complete one.

25. Never fall asleep in class.

A great way to get on your professor's bad side is to let them know you think they're boring.

If you're ever so tired that you fall asleep in class, make sure you don't make a scene. My sophomore year of college, I was in a Geography class with theatre style seating and those annoying wooden mini-tables attached to each chair. As I was coloring in the eastern coast of Africa in my notes, I nodded out. I fell into a deep sleep. A few minutes later, I scared myself awake, jumping like I had just seen a ghost in my own bedroom. Besides the fact that the people sitting next to me noticed I jumped frantically, I also snapped my neck and knocked all the books and colored pencils off the mini-table. My neck felt liked it got cranked by a UFC fighter, and I may have been a bit embarrassed. The takeaway? Walk out.

26. Declare a major by your third year.

Or you begin to risk wasting a lot of time and money taking classes that could be pointless in the long run.

27. Schedule labs for the morning.

This ensures all materials are in stock.

28. Learn the names of your professors.

It's common courtesy to be able to refer to somebody as their name, not just their title.

29. Offer to quiz fellow students before taking a test.

Asking questions and hearing the answers is a great way to internalize info.

30. Don't write in red ink.

It's displeasing to the eye.

31. Be the one to write the lab report.

You never want your name on anything written by someone else.

32. Ask your professor's advice on choosing interesting classes.

A lot of times, all it takes for a class to be interesting is an enthusiastic professor. Or you can just ask them, "Who is the loudest professor in the break room?"

33. When corresponding with professors, stay professional and don't use slang terms.

Even if your professor acts unprofessionally, keep your composure.

During my junior year, I had this awesome professor who was fresh out of grad school and maybe five years older than me. One evening, I walked into a local grill and bar and heard my nickname shouted out by some drunk dude. I looked over my left shoulder, and it was my professor who was blitzed out of his gourd. I talked to him and his wife for a few minutes, and he insisted on buying me a drink. Although I wanted a free drink and to laugh hysterically at him, I refused the drink and never lost composure. When I saw him in class after that, I never mentioned it. He probably wouldn't remember this unless I reminded him, and I could've held it over him forever, but staying respectful netted me the best reference letter anyone could write. The takeaway? If you see a professor or boss anywhere, just leave.

34. See a free tutor if you need help.

Talk to your counselor or academic advisor about your options.

35. Go to every test review you can.

If you go to all of them, you may hear the answer to every question.

36. Raise your hand in class before speaking.

Even if it isn't a classroom rule, it's courteous and lets everyone know you want to speak.

37. Bring water to class.

Sipping water helps keep you awake, alert, and hydrated.

38. Never print anything that can be copied.

Copy machine ink is cheaper and less wasteful than most printers. If you need five copies of the same paper, print one and make four copies.

39. If cheat sheets are allowed on tests, write small.

You can fit far more words on a page when you type them versus write them, plus, they are way easier to read. If your notes are handwritten, consider transferring them to a computer.

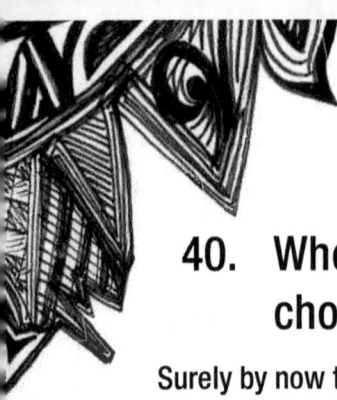

40. When in doubt on a multiple choice test, answer B.

Surely by now they know we always guess answer C.

Tests are way more personal than you think. An exam is a battle of you versus someone who wants to know if you listen to them. Tests sometimes have patterns and nuances that reveal the correct answer. Unfortunately, I didn't notice this until I had my last test in History of the American West. The professor had placed a period at the end of three of the four possible choices on every set of responses. I knew this couldn't be a coincidence, so I answered every question with whatever choice didn't have a period. I aced the test. As both a student and a teacher, I've witnessed and used the easiest way to answer a student's question on a test: give them the answer key. If you're taking a multiple choice test, look for consistencies in capitalization of the first word in the answer, punctuation near the end of the sentence, and even punctuation after the option. These are all used as professor tricks. The takeaway? Go through your test for a few minutes before touching your pen.

41. Try taking an online class.

They aren't for everyone, but a lot of time and money can be saved by taking classes from home. Because it takes so much independent work, consider only taking online classes in your strongest areas.

42. Don't fan yourself in a hot classroom.

You'll make yourself hotter in the long run, and whichever hand you fan with will have swampy underarm, visible from a mile away.

43. If you talk about illegal activities in front of your professor, they may be obligated to report it.

Just because the person has a doctorate doesn't mean you get doctor/client privilege; zip it.

44. Eat tuna fish.

This is probably the cheapest and best way to spike brain flow before quizzes, tests, and speeches.

45. Don't show your grade to other students unless they've asked or already shown you their grade.

Don't assume people want to share in your glory or your defeat. Admire that A and sit there like a champ.

46. Don't attempt cramming.

Unless your middle name is Clutch, and you know you can pull it off.

47. Write your own test review.

Not everyone has the same notetaking style, and you could end up trying to read something that looks more like art.

48. Judge classes by their name.

If it sounds boring, it is boring.

49. Don't crack your knuckles, back, or any other joints in class.

Yuck.

50. If you mess up typing a paper, try hitting CTRL + Z.

This is the quickest way to undo any bad thing you have ever done. Well, for the most part.

51. Take classes that double dip.

There are some classes that not only count towards your major, but also fulfill other requirements for graduation. Make sure you ask your counselor what's what.

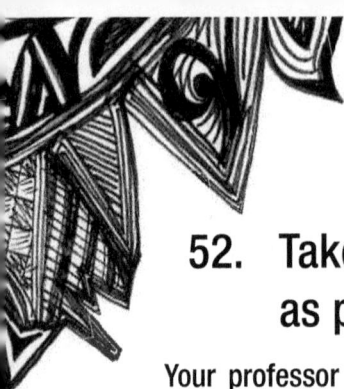

52. Take classes as early as possible.

Your professor is usually in the best mood when they haven't seen enough people to annoy them yet.

One of the coolest and most influential professors I've had was for a class that took place from 7-8:15 am. We wrote a lot of papers in that class, and he was an avid reader and responder. When he returned your paper, he had usually written more words in his comments and reactions than you did on the paper—a great reassurance that he was reading every word I had written. Every once in a while when we arrived at class, his daughter would be sleeping on the table in the back of the room. He was always laid back, as long as we didn't wake her. He would also bring us chocolate milk and mini donuts if we did well. I had the pleasure of running into him a few semesters later while he was preparing for another class. I stopped to tell him how much I enjoyed his class and how much I learned from him. Hilariously, he had no idea who I was. The takeaway? Don't bug professors in the middle of their day.

53. Never try to be the first to finish a test.

Hopefully you got over this in grade school, but if not, find something else to win at.

54. Take advantage of pass/fail classes.

There are professors who still grade pass/fail. This is an easy credit; just make sure you show up and participate. Done and done.

55. Don't use whiteout on anything you submit.

Don't be lazy. Fix it on the computer and reprint it.

56. Avoid the word "um" when speaking in front of others.

It's just proof you didn't think before speaking.

57. Don't click your pen in class.

If you're one of those people who gets fidgety, always use an old-school pen with a cap.

58. Submit papers with your last name on every page.

It helps the professor out and it helps keep your ideas yours.

59. Always check for assignments online.

A lot of professors get their assignments from the internet, and many times the answer key is out there too.

60. Ask the professor to see examples of essays before writing your own.

Essays can be worth as much as tests, so this is basically like getting the professor to show you the answer key before a multiple choice exam.

61. Try to sit in the front row.

A professor's likelihood to place a good grade next to your name goes up if they can put a face with that name.

This is a tip you should think about every time you go to class. Someone who sits in the front row gets an automatic nod as someone who cares. Now, I'm not saying you need to sit in the front row all the time, just enough to get your face and name recognized. If there's a day you think you may fall asleep, don't sit in the front row. If there's a day you think you'll be texting or on your phone a lot, don't sit in the front row. I had a professor with whom I thought I had a good relationship. One day, as I sat in the front row, she stopped mid-lecture, stared deep into my soul, and said to me, as I was texting, "Your cell phone is going to be the death of you." The takeaway? Only sit in the front row if you're going to be attentive and involved.

Add your own tip or artwork.

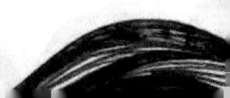

CLOSE QUARTERS

Dorm living and keeping the peace with your roommates.

Depending on your childhood, you may have never shared a room, elbow to elbow, with anyone other than a close relative. Prepare yourself. Your patience will be tested and your things may get lost, but most things can be replaced. Your focus should be on creating lifelong memories of fun and friendship and learning who you are as a person. Also, never underestimate the importance of a good night's sleep.

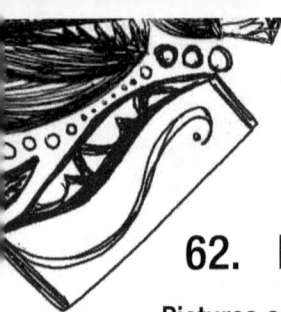

62. Decorate your dorm room.

Pictures are a great way to display your personality, and you can hide things behind them.

One of my friends lived in a cookie-cutter style dorm room that had these cheap shelves built directly into the wall. The rooms had no cabinets with doors on them for privacy. Thinking outside the box, we bought a large picture to hang over the shelves to hide anything we didn't want to share or have seen. Lots of people came into that room and commented on how it was odd that there were no shelves like there were in all the other rooms, even the RA mentioned it. Not once did any of them ever stop to think that the picture was simply covering them up. Out of sight. Out of mind. The takeaway? Spice up your room with elements of your personality and think outside the box; decorations can be functional as well.

63. Trust no one.

Write your name on everything you own. It helps protect your stuff, and it's also funny to see how your handwriting changes over the years.

64. Own at least one set of your own dishes.

You know how your roommate says they wash their dishes every time? They don't.

65. Don't think you have to be your roommate's best friend.

It's pretty tough to complain about your roommate to your roommate, isn't it?

66. Spend at least an hour per day outside your dorm room and not in a class.

A breath of fresh air is the most important of all breaths.

67. Invest in a shower caddy.

So if your loofah gets moldy, at least it's your mold. Seriously, get a new loofah or wash cloth regularly.

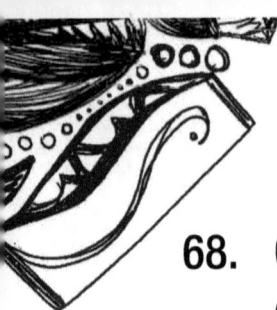

68. Close the blinds in your dorm room at night.

On campus, there are way too many lights around to get a good night's sleep. If your eyes are closing, make your room as dark as possible.

69. Don't fall asleep around your friends.

Or expect a Facebook album with your face as a graffiti wall. This didn't happen to me personally, but a guy I know.

70. Go to your roommate's hometown at least once.

There is no way to truly know someone until you've seen where they were raised and met their weird family.

71. Make popcorn in a neighbor's room.

Unless you have the cooking time down to a science. It's best to turn popcorn black in a place you don't have to sleep.

72. Use liquid soap.

Bar soap is easily dropped, and it sits out, dries up, and collects nasties.

When I was a freshman, I tried to use the soap the school provided in the locker room showers. Within a couple days, my skin looked like I was a reptile, so I started bringing my own bottle of that fancy shampoo/conditioner/body wash in one. One day, when I got to the locker room, I opened my gym bag and the cap had broken. What I thought was a good deal ended up being thirty-two ounces of soap on the inside of a small gym bag. This is when I got the idea to buy my shampoo, conditioner, and body wash in bulk to save money, but to fill small bottles with it to ensure I didn't lose it all at once if I dropped it or the cap broke. The takeaway? Buy small reusable bottles and fill them up yourself.

73. Lock your dorm room.

Things will go missing. Most of the time, you just forgot where you put something, but you can seriously narrow down the number of suspects if you just lock your door.

74. Don't go anywhere barefoot.

Inside at least. Dorm floors are a breeding ground for bacteria. Don't kick your shoes off until you're outdoors.

75. Don't trash talk your roommate to anyone but your own mother.

Also keep in mind that you shouldn't talk behind the back of someone who sleeps near you.

76. Keep your toothbrush covered when not in use.

Germs aside, one careless spray of perfume or cologne gives your brush a horrendous new taste.

77. Ask your roommate before inviting a guest to stay over.

Especially if that guest is a parent or love interest.

78. Don't throw wet towels on the floor.

They are easily forgotten and get nasty quickly.

79. Close your eyes to let them adjust to the dark.

It sounds stupid, but it works.

80. Don't jump on your bed unless your roommate does too.

That way you have someone to blame it on.

81. Keep music at a moderate volume.

Or blast it as loud as you want in your headphones.

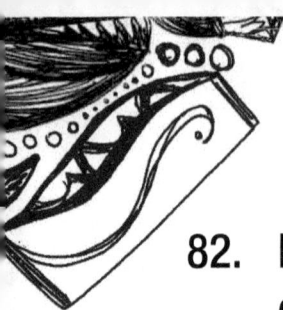

82. Don't get involved in any drama on your floor.

Everyone will pick a side, and all of a sudden you'll be involved in a popularity contest.

Now I'm not pointing fingers here, but most of the dorm drama I witnessed involved photos on Facebook. One time, a very jealous girl noticed her boyfriend was tagged in a photo with another girl who lived across the hall. The funny thing was, the couple worked together, and the boyfriend had called in sick to work that night. He apparently went to a party with the girl in the picture. For the next six weeks, I got to see live action reality TV. The girls on that floor became so engrossed in the battle between bitter beauties. Not only did they pick sides, they gave their new found groups names, and even made t-shirts with the names on them. It was probably the most ridiculous thing I'd ever seen. The takeaway? Change your Facebook setting to "approve all posts."

83. Don't leave underwear lying around your room.

Not only is it bad for cleanliness, your RA doesn't need to know what's under your jeans.

84. Make sure your power strips have surge protectors.

This is a cheap insurance policy on your electronics.

85. Suck up to the RA.

Seriously, this is a must. Whether you're locked out of your room or need to beg them not to call campus security, you'll want them on your side.

86. Make sure you can close your closet door.

Open doors are inviting. The best way to keep your roommate from wearing all of your clothes is simply keeping your clothes out of their view.

87. Know your roommate's least favorite color.

This one is simply for torment, and so you can buy things they never want to borrow.

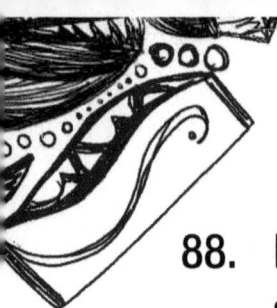

88. Keep your room key in the same place.

This will prevent you from having to look for it every time you leave your room, and lots of dorm room doors lock automatically.

89. Know that your dorm can be searched at any time.

It's not your dorm; it's the school's, and they have the right to see what you're keeping in there.

90. Memorize the names of people who live near you.

91. If you get angry at your roommate, go for a walk.

Just lock up your valuables and leave.

92. Own an Ethernet cable.

Dorms are notorious for having bad wireless internet. When your reception is bad, just hardwire it.

93. Make your roommate's birthday special for them.

They will never forget it.

94. Buy a trashcan that doesn't have holes in it.

It's likely you'll be eating in your room, and chances are likely you're using a grocery bag for a trashcan liner, and those things leak.

95. Know the cleaning times of your dorm's bathrooms.

You're not allowed to enter at these times, and you want to be sure you have enough time to go to a bathroom on *another* floor so you don't go to the bathroom *on* the floor.

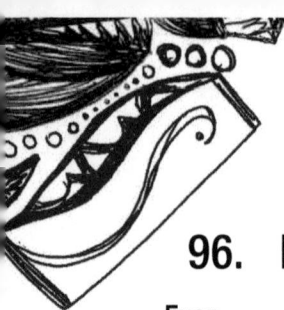

96. Don't burn candles.

Ever.

Even if candles don't catch something on fire, the small amount of smoke they emit, especially when extinguished, is enough to set off sensitive fire alarms in dorms. One night while I was actually getting some sleep for a change, some genius couple decided they wanted a romantic, candle-lit night. What they got was a dorm full of angry students in their pajamas standing on the curb with them in ten-degree weather while the firefighters searched the building, room by room, making sure everyone had evacuated. I knew the people who did it, and I still haven't forgiven them. The takeaway? Don't try to be romantic in a dorm.

PARTY LIFE

Being the life of the party and
not making yourself look stupid.

Partying in college will make life interesting. Friends will be made, friendships will end, and people will show you their true colors. Whether you're the type of person who likes to host or the type who prefers to skip from party to party, always be safe, plan ahead, and watch out for the other guy.

97. Never wear white to a jungle juice party.

Never wear white to any party, really. You're there to meet people. No one introduces their friends to someone with a stain on their shirt.

I was at a jungle juice party, old school style, with the juice in the laundry room. As soon as I got a refill, I took a rough shoulder to my drinking arm and spilled the juice all over me. I was faced with three options: 1) Act like nothing happened and keep wearing the shirt. 2) Take the shirt off. 3) Dump juice on the rest of the shirt to turn the whole thing red. I opted to take my shirt off. At the time, I was about 140 pounds soaking wet— not exactly a muscle man. Another guy at the party was though. He thought I was taking my shirt off to show off my noodle arms, so he decided to take his shirt off too. The next thing I knew, all these random guys took their shirts off to impress the ladies there. I didn't last long in that environment; my friends and I left for another party. When we got there, I had no choice but to wear my juice-stained shirt. One of my friends found it hilarious to introduce me to people and then ask them if they have any shout wipes. The takeaway? If something like this happens to you, you could write a book.

98. Never go to parties alone.

For reasons why, watch every creepy movie ever.

99. Line up a safe ride home.

This is the most important plan you make.

100. Never tell anyone what you're afraid of.

The surefire way to be the butt end of pranks is to let your friends in on what your biggest fears and phobias are.

101. If you play a pong game at a party, drink out of your own cup, not the ones being used for the game.

Even if you're using new cups, tread lightly. Most of the germs are on the ping pong balls. Research shows ping pong balls used for beer pong can contain both salmonella and e-coli. They can also carry over two million other bacteria per ball.

102. Tip the delivery guy.

Very few times in your life can a few bucks change someone's mood; don't be cheap.

103. Spout off random facts at social gatherings.

Then let everyone know that 85% of facts are made up.

104. Never accept a drink if you don't know its origin.

Anything in closed cans or bottles is usually safe.

105. Know the words to popular songs.

More than likely they'll be played at parties, and you can lead the karaoke scene.

This can be a touchy one. If you're at a party where everyone is into it, join in. I remember being at a party that turned from a group-sing into a very competitive singing contest. Since my friend started the singing, he thought he was a great candidate for karaoke. He wasn't. Despite being the fist-pumping all-star he was when everyone was singing with him, solo, he was nothing more than an off-key chump. All night long. The takeaway? If you're singing, make sure you hear pitch, not feel it.

106. Don't run down the stairs.

Unless you want the stairway to be named in your memory.

107. Don't do things simply to annoy people.

No matter how funny you think it is. Picking at people is classless, and everyone else sees it.

108. Don't use lame pickup lines.

In a few situations, they can be funny, but usually you just look like a person with nothing better to say.

109. Offer strangers a piece of gum.

And if they refuse, you can say, "Good. I didn't want to share anyway."

110. Know that everything you say will be used against you.

Not only in a court of law, but even with your ride-til-ya-die homies.

111. Never wear new shoes to a party.

Obviously, there's a spill risk, but at college parties, there's also a dingy floor risk. Those new kicks will sound sticky with every step for two weeks.

112. Don't fall asleep with your shoes on.

This is a very strict fraternity party rule. If you fall asleep with your shoes on, you're basically a sidewalk and all your friends are the chalk.

This one has definitely bitten me in the rear; not every party abides by frat rules. I went to a party with a "friend" of mine, and as soon as we arrived, they noticed their pending significant-other was there. I played it right and faded into the distance. I found a couch and took off my shoes. My legs were crossed and I had my hat down over my eyes like a cowboy. The next thing I knew there were things being broken all around me and a golf club-wielding pip squeak was chasing me out the door. Thankfully, I remembered to grab my shoes. The takeaway? Never fall asleep at random places.

113. Pretend you don't know the chicken dance, if asked.

But if everyone else is doing it, it's okay to join in.

114. Don't hate.

Not only is it none of your business, you just come off as jealous.

115.   Practice your laugh.

Or you'll end up as a vine.

116.   Memorize the alphabet backwards.

Not only can this help you get out of trouble, but you might just impress a new friend.

117.   Chip in for gas money.

Ever wonder how people decide who the odd one out is? It wasn't the one who chipped in for gas.

118. Never carry more than fifty dollars in cash.

The only options with cash are spending it, keeping it, losing it, and having it stolen. Three out of the four are bad.

Even though leaving your money behind is a good idea, make sure you store it in a safe place. One weekend, I worked some overtime as a bar-back and actually ended up making quite a bit of money. One night when we were heading out, I took all that money out of my wallet and walked out the door with forty bucks. The next morning, I couldn't find my money anywhere. I did my best to not point fingers at all of my friends who had been in my room the night before, but it was very difficult not to. After a week of being a grouch over losing my money, I finally decided I could be around my friends again. I put on my lucky green shirt and grabbed my green shoes. I couldn't get my left foot in because something was in my shoe. I reached in and pulled out the $279 I made as a bar-back. I also had to buy for my friends that night to apologize for being a chump. The takeaway? Have a safe place to stash your valuables.

Add your own tip or artwork.

AROUND CAMPUS

The things you need to know that couldn't be categorized.

Here are some things that won't necessarily be used every day, maybe not even in a class or at a party. These are the things that fall between the cracks of daily thought and are impossible to learn without having experienced them. Thanks to the modern technology of the printing press, you can become aware beforehand.

119. Don't tell too many high school stories.

From this day forward, it's about tomorrow; no one cares about your yesterday.

In less harsh terms, focus on tomorrow. I can take you back to the first time I ever witnessed someone being curbed. I was working as the assistant to a great baseball hitting instructor. One day, he gave this junior in college some advice and the kid replied, "Funny, I've never been told to change that before, and I led the team in hitting last year." The coach, who was five feet, six inches tall, quipped back, "And I was the tallest kid in fifth grade. Who cares?" The takeaway? Realize the reason you enrolled in college is because you care about the rest of your life, not just what you've already done.

120. Make friends with an upperclassman.

From potential professors to parties and partners, an upperclassman who's a close friend is nearly irreplaceable.

121. Go out of your way to greet people you recognize.

Even if it's just some random person from history class, you never know when you'll run into them again.

122. Attend a game for each sport at least once.

Not only does it show support for your school, but the games are usually a lot of fun and a great way to meet people.

123. Never park illegally.

Save yourself a lot of time, money, and embarrassment by just staying between the lines. The campus security hero has his eye on you. By the way, unpaid fines can prevent you from enrolling in classes—or even graduating.

124. Never buy anything but books at your bookstore, and even books should be a last resort.

College bookstores are a prime spot for huge price mark ups. You'll go in to buy Dad a hat and come out with $9 batteries and a $30 phone charger with your mascot on it.

125. Don't limit yourself to high school friends.

Branch out and meet new people. Plus, new friends have less dirt on you.

126. Stay in touch with high school teachers.

Can you say reference letter? A high school teacher's recommendation and a college professor's good word show dedication and consistency in behavior.

127. Don't drink too much caffeine.

If you want it to work on demand, then you can't overuse it.

128. Establish a routine for charging your laptop, phone, and other electronics.

Think about investing in a portable power source so you're never left disconnected.

129. Be extra nice to dining hall workers.

They work as hard as anyone else around campus and they decide how much food you get!

A girl I dated went to a really expensive private school that had a lunch buffet to match. The problem was it cost thirteen bucks for people who didn't go to that school. I reluctantly paid the thirteen dollars and made small talk with the guy who worked the cash drawer. From that day on, any time I paid him for the buffet, he'd just give me my money back after fumbling in the cash register to make it look like he was giving me change. He never made me pay for the buffet again. The takeaway? Keep a smile on your face, and the world will have your back.

130. Apply for every scholarship out there.

Just because you've already started college doesn't mean you can't get another scholarship next year.

131. When someone mentions the starting quarterback, pretend you don't know his name.

Whether you're a man or woman, you don't want to come off as a jersey chaser.

132. Don't allow yourself an excuse to start smoking.

If you hang around people who smoke, they only want you to start smoking so they can eventually bum some off of you.

133. Memorize your student ID number.

This is your bloodline on campus. Many schools allow you to access everything from your library card to your bank account by using your student ID number.

134. Always offer help to someone who looks confused.

135. Bookmark useful websites.

Most browsers these days save your most visited sites, but you'll want to have the best translators and measurement converters at your fingertips.

136. Learn your way around the student union.

From restaurants to charging stations, you'll never know when you'll have to make a quick stop in that ten minute break between classes.

137. Read the school newspaper.

Even if you just browse through it quickly, take a gander. It's a great resource to find events happening around campus. If you can't find a hard copy, try looking online.

138. Never loan money to a friend or classmate.

Not for pop, lunch, or books. Never. It's awkward having to cave in knee caps for the price of a chocolate muffin.

A friend of mine loaned another buddy a couple hundred bucks when he was in a serious pickle. They had agreed the loan would be paid back within one month. Things were normal between the friends during that month, but at the end of the month, the loan had not been repaid. Not even a dime. As the days went on, every time we were all together, you could tell there was tension between the two of them, especially on days when we went out to eat and the guy who borrowed the money was spending it like it was going out of style. The takeaway? Never loan money unless there's an emergency. Regardless of how little the loan is, have the terms of the loan in writing.

139. Learn the names of the university's shuttle drivers.

This may be the closest you ever get to a personal driver and a limo.

140. Check your email every chance you get.

Assuming you don't already. Classes are cancelled more than you think, and this prevents a half-mile trek across campus.

141. Own at least one pair of sunglasses.

If it's not the sun in your eyes, it'll be a late night and an eight a.m. class. Either way, you'll want a pair.

142. Let someone know if you're walking someplace alone.

It sounds tacky, but who wants to end up with a creepy, low-budget documentary about them?

143. Never borrow money from a friend or classmate.

Not for pop, lunch, or books. Never. School probably has you in enough debt; the last thing you need is a friend over your shoulder for sixty cents.

144. Buy reusable shopping bags.

From holding books to dirty laundry, they're useful for much more than groceries.

145. Never be the first to re-enter a building after a fire drill.

This one is no joke. Unfortunately, campuses can be dangerous. Someone gets paid to be the guy to go in first; let them do it.

146. Don't wear your high school letter jacket around campus.

Unless you're about to freeze to death.

147. Don't download music on campus, legally or illegally.

Just don't do it. Besides, it takes forever.

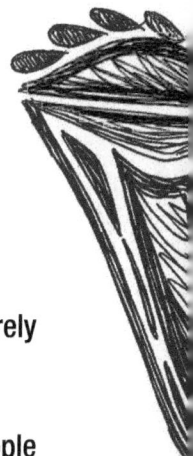

148. Check your pockets before washing your clothes.

Then double check them. Community washers rarely give back.

It's not the washers who are the culprits, it's the people who get into them. I had a friend who was known for her hilarious choices on the socks she wore. One day, she was wearing some that were so mismatched, I had to comment. I asked her how she decided to wear those socks today. Her response was, "I didn't have any clean ones and these were the first out of the far left dryer on my floor." The takeaway? Only wash clothes if you're going to be there to dry them and take them out of the dryer. To avoid losing socks, put them in a small mesh bag and include them in your normal load of laundry.

149. Wherever you're going, smile, smile, smile.

People will either think you're happy or that you're keeping a secret. Either way, they want to know why.

150. Keep an extra pair of headphones around.

Your headphones might quit working, or you could even make a new friend by loaning them out.

151. Read a book with tips for surviving college.

Congrats; you're on the way!

152. Know where to find the nearest grocery store.

The cheapest place to get food is as close to the source as possible. If you're pinching pennies, stay away from prepared food and do the work yourself.

153. Never try dating the same person twice.

It's never as good as it once was, and people don't change.

154. Don't get a job you can't walk to, unless you own your own car.

Your job depends on you; you shouldn't depend on someone else to get you there.

155. Know the number to campus security.

Although their flashlights may not look like a weapon, their radios are, and they can get you help quickly. If you are on the accused end of it, know you can never outrun radio waves.

156. Never sign up for anything free.

Nothing is ever really free, and your cell phone will blow up with more "free" offers.

157. Learn the seven deadly sins.

In college, you'll fall victim to each one at least once. It's up to you to prevent how far you fall.

If you don't know the seven deadly sins, they are: pride, greed, lust, envy, gluttony, wrath, and sloth. The "freshmen fifteen" is a real thing. Gluttony will be the toughest of the seven sins to avoid for most people. My freshman year, I caved to gluttony and, after a very long night, ventured to a local late-night restaurant to indulge. After I ordered my burger and a heaping pile of tater tots, I was visited by the heavyset manager of the restaurant. He told me he gave me extra tots because I always made him laugh in high school, but he was unrecognizable to me. After scanning my brain, I realized he was the really ripped guy in my weightlifting class in high school. I should've learned the lesson immediately, but instead I thanked him for the extra tots and ate every last one. Feeling guilty, I worked out hardcore the next day. The takeaway? Come to grips with knowing that, as an adult, every decision has potentially life-changing consequences, even if that decision is only worth a few hundred calories.

158. Keep a calendar.

Electronic or paper—know what's up!

159. Never leave your laptop open.

It wastes energy and kills privacy.

160. Take a world religions class.

Not only will it increase knowledge, but it will also increase your understanding of other religions and cultures.

161. Wash your hands or use hand sanitizer after using a campus computer.

The next Ebola scare lives there.

162. Wear your school's colors to class on Fridays.

This may have stuck with you since spirit day in elementary school. Wearing the same colors as the people around you creates a sense of unity and pride.

163. Go somewhere for spring break at least once.

Go there, enjoy it, and never speak of it again.

164. Don't wear your jeans more than three times without washing them.

They may look good to you, but to us they look funky and a bit too big.

165. Buy a meal plan.

It saves big bucks in the long run, and there's usually something open on campus when hunger strikes.

166. If you get lost, ask for directions.

Holding on to a little pride isn't worth being late for class. Besides, you may learn an awesome shortcut you can use at other times too.

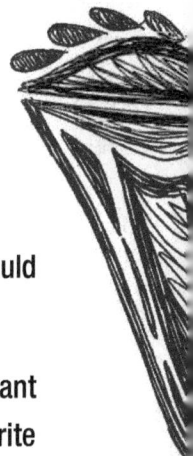

167. Learn how to sew.

Even if you can't fix a tear in your suit or dress, you should at least be able to sew a button back on.

One night, I was laying out my clothes for a very important presentation the next day. When I was ironing my favorite dress shirt, I noticed the button just below my collar was missing. I didn't have the money or time to run out and get a new shirt, nor did I want to show up to class with my top two buttons undone, like a mobster. I needed to learn how to sew on a button. My dad knew the basic steps, but neither one of us even knew how to thread a needle. He told me we needed to ask my mom, but there was one problem: not only was she out of town, she wasn't even in the United States, or on our continent. My dad made it happen though. He left a message at the hotel to have my mom call me. About forty minutes before I had to present, my phone rang, and it was my mom. At 4:40 pm Israel time, my mom taught me how to sew on a button for a 9:00am class. The takeaway? If you don't know how to sew, at least be able to get a hold of your mom.

168. Never refer to anyone as an ethnic slur.

No matter how long you've known them or how much you're joking. Just because someone is okay with being called that, doesn't mean other people are okay with hearing it.

169. Clean out your backpack every day.

Otherwise, you'll end up on the show *Hoarders: College Edition*.

170. Learn how to change a tire.

So if you get a boot put on your car for parking illegally, you can just take off the whole tire and put your spare on. Don't tell anyone we told you this one.

171. Never walk in the grass on campus.

This not only shows a lack of respect for your school, but also for the people who keep the campus looking pretty.

172. Take the stairs whenever possible.

Help slow down the obesity monster.

173. Match your underwear to whatever shirt you are wearing.

No matter how bad things get some days, hey, at least your shirt matches your underpants.

174. Don't call people stupid and don't tell people to shut up.

You should know this by now, but some people never forget being insulted.

175. Work at a restaurant for at least two months.

You will have much more respect for restaurant workers in the future and hopefully won't be such a cheapskate when tipping.

176. Don't wear slippers and act like they're shoes.

You can tell a lot about a person by their shoes, and slippers say, "I'm here, but I don't care about anything."

I had a very pretentious professor in Economics my sophomore year. There was a girl in my class who was very intelligent. She asked amazing questions that always seemed to be whatever everyone in the class was thinking. The problem was, she always showed up in slippers. No matter how good of a question she asked, the professor always responded to her with a chuckle and a sarcastic answer. After listening to his rudeness, another student would basically rephrase the question. To that student, the professor was on point and serious. To this day, I know it was because she always wore slippers. The takeaway? If you care enough to go to class, care enough to dress appropriately.

177. Pick a twelve seed over a five seed.

March Madness, baby!

178. Never talk badly about your school's band.

They bring more energy to games than you realize.

179. Read a book at least once a year.

Something that you chose to read on your own, and the back of a shampoo bottle doesn't count.

180. Always go to your school's tournament or playoff games.

Show some school spirit, and if they win, hopefully you remember it.

181. Don't go to seminars on campus.

Lured in by the free pizza? It actually costs you the hour and a half of listening to that bald dude ramble.

182. Take a foreign language class.

It doesn't matter which language, but it will help you understand your native language at a more in-depth level.

183. Make sure you use the proper forms of your and you're.

Or your going to look dumb. (Yes, that's intentional, and if you didn't get the joke, keep practicing.)

184. Make sure tuition is paid on time.

Otherwise, holds can be put on your account, transcripts can be frozen, and your school mascot will deliver a giant red letter while you're in class.

185. Have stamps on hand.

You'll need one eventually, and so will a friend, even though they'll make fun of you for carrying stamps afterwards.

One of my best friends from college was one of those people who always took things too seriously. On a random Wednesday, he was so panicked his face was changing colors. He had a bill due in two days and he hadn't mailed it yet. All the post offices were already closed, and he really wanted to get it put in the mail that night. We found out the post office at the airport operated twenty four hours per day, and that if he brought it down it could still be post marked on that day. When we got down there, we found out they only received packages to ship, but provided no other services, like selling stamps! Just then, I remembered I had a booklet of eight forever stamps in my wallet that had literally been there since high school. I offered my panicked friend that stamp, he accepted, and without skipping a beat, made fun of me for being like an old man that carried stamps in his wallet. The takeaway? Realize no good deed goes unpunished.

186. If you're ever going to write a paper for someone else, make sure you get paid in advance.

Now, now, you shouldn't be doing this anyway, but if you do, make sure you look for a paper on the internet before writing it yourself.

187. Try to take Fridays off.

Thursday and Friday are the new Friday and Saturday.

188. Shy away from microwaveable meals.

It's okay to eat them every once in a while between classes, but all of the sodium and preservatives may leave you feeling lethargic and worthless.

189. Don't pick your nose.

In front of others.

190. Don't walk faster than your feet can move.

Otherwise your knee caps will match your red shirt.

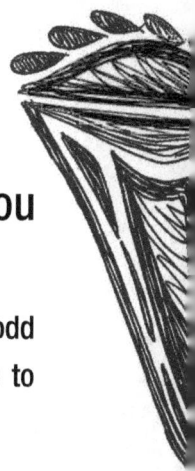

191. Memorize the TV channels you regularly watch.

The campus rec and the dorms are known for odd programming. Make a cheat sheet for the channels to avoid watching all infomercials.

192. If you don't know, just ask.

Despite what the news shows, there are still good people in the world. If you need help, ask someone who looks friendly; they usually are.

193. Send your parents postcards from campus.

It's rumored that every postcard mom and dad receive is worth $20 in groceries.

194. Be honest with yourself.

From how much money you have to how long it takes to get ready in the morning. It's easy to lie to other people, but you have to go really low to lie to yourself.

195. Buy things with $2 bills.

They're a conversation starter, and we must do our duty to recirculate them.

If you can believe it, there are some people who have never seen a $2 bill; I hope you're not one of those people. During my sophomore year, I went on a small trip with a few of my friends, and we were shopping at Mall of America. It was nearing the end of the trip, and my budget was running low. I found a pair of shorts on clearance for $19.99. In my wallet, I had a $20 bill and a $2 bill. I knew the two bucks would be enough for tax, so I proceeded to the check out. When I got to the checkout, the young cashier said, "I'm sorry; I can't accept this $2 bill." I asked why not, and she replied, "Because there is no such thing as a $2 bill." I laughed and assured her there was. She then told me she would go get her manager if I didn't leave the store. I asked her to please get the manager because I really wanted to buy these shorts, and, surely her manager had seen a $2 bill, or at least knew they existed. She called the manager on her headset, and he came storming out. He yanked his headset off and put it around his neck like a football coach about to give a referee an earful. He snatched the $2 bill and twenty from her hands, wrinkled it in his hands like trash, and yelled, "If you don't leave this store with your fake money, I'm going to call the police." The takeaway? Never overestimate human intelligence, even if they are a manager.

196. Know the words to your school song.

This will come in handy more times than you could ever imagine.

197. If you ride a bike, lock it up.

Or be prepared to pay forty dollars for it at the local pawn shop.

198. Carry hand sanitizer.

Keep in mind, thousands of people have touched that door handle today.

199. Don't wear nice shoes in the rain.

And if your "nice shoes" are waterproof, never wear them.

200. Check for toilet paper before... you know.

You don't want to get caught brown-handed.

201. Don't use automatic door openers unless you have to.

They do have a limited number of uses before they need to be serviced and there are people who actually need them.

202. Ask before changing the channel on a community TV.

Or just wear a shirt that says, "I think I'm more important than everyone else."

203. Be polite to everyone.

You do not have to respect someone who hasn't earned it, but you should always be polite.

204. Know the names of some local bands.

Not only is it fun to check out a local show, but they might be the next big thing, and you can say you found them first.

My sophomore year of college, I went to a local show with my sister and a few friends. We went there to see the headliner, but as we arrived, the opening band was on stage, and they were killing it. At the time, I really hadn't seen a local act that impressed me the way Screaming for Silence did. One of my friends ended up doing some marketing for them and later on, I had the pleasure of getting to hang out with them and even play a little music. A conversation with one of their guitar players convinced me that you actually can do anything you want in this world. Although I'd heard this before, he was showing me, not just telling me. It was this conversation that ultimately got me into writing. Since then, I've watched them grow from a local band of a few friends into an award-winning band you can hear on many stations and satellite radio. The takeaway? Always be open to different sources of inspiration. Something that seems like a small conversation at one time, can actually be a life changer.

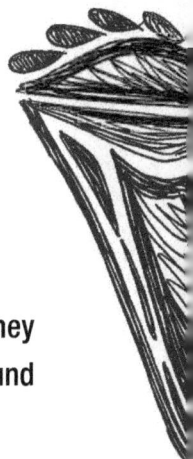

Add your own tip or artwork.

BONUS LIFE TIPS

Things that may not apply directly to college, but you'll need for life.

When this book was being written, there were exactly 500 tips. These are all the extra tips that got cut for not applying to a chapter, being outdated, or getting labeled "weird advice." However, that doesn't mean they aren't true.

205. Arguing with someone you know will never change their mind is a fruitless pursuit.

The toughest idea I've ever had to grasp was that arguing with someone was my own fault. Anytime I ever argued with someone was because I was trying to convince them of something, or as I saw it, teach them something. The more I came across stubborn people, the more I found myself coming up with retorts that only I could understand. After a few sessions of yelling at the same guy, I realized there was no changing his mind. There was no convincing him of anything, no matter how much proof I showed him. It dawned on me that the arguments were my fault. I knew going into the battle that this guy would never comprehend what I was saying, yet I still talked myself blue in the face trying to teach him. The takeaway?

If you continue on with someone who won't change their mind, you aren't fighting them, you're fighting your own ego.

206. Carry extra change in your pocket and think big coins. From tax to nominal printing charges, I'd rather carry four quarters than weigh myself down with ten nickels, sixteen pennies, and a tiny dime.

207. Invest in a bicycle or other alternate modes of transportation.

208. Have access to a mini stapler.

209. Supplement notes with a highlighter.

210. Take to-go bags to buffets.

211. Have access to a refrigerator.

212. Own a pair of scissors.

213. Call your parents at least twice a week. (Tell your parents this should be number one and a safe ride home number two out of the five hundred.)

214. Wake up ten minutes before you think you have to. If you don't have to be up at a certain time, sleep ten minutes longer than you think you need to.

215. Lay out your clothes the night before.

216. Get at least six hours of sleep.

217. Hand-written notes should be taken in pencil.

218. Try eating cheap noodles with butter, cinnamon, and sugar for a nice change.

219. Buy a reusable water bottle.

220. Brush your teeth before bedtime.

221. Take the comforter off your bed before you clean your dorm room. This will help prevent your bed from becoming the catchall of your random things and will also prevent nasty dust from gathering on your bedspread.

222. Always wear clean socks.

223. Have access to fresh fruit.

224. Know the name of the dean of your college.

225. Set at least two alarms.

226. Join a club or group.

227. Help out with community service in your college's surrounding area.

228. Wear comfortable shoes to class.

229. Have a least three shirts with your university's name on it.

230. Try playing Ultimate Frisbee.

231. Do your best to not join a politically affiliated group. Politics or religion—stay away.

232. Wash your face
every morning.

233. Always refer to people with
doctorates as doctor, even if
they tell you not to.

234. Don't keep more than
fifteen shirts.

235. Get to know your academic
advisor.

236. Charge your cell phone
every night.

237. Have access to an
ice machine.

238. Workout at least three times
a week.

239. Don't eat after nine p.m.

240. Do something nice for another student once a week.

241. Don't eat pizza more than three times in a week.

242. Look for coupons in a local newspaper.

243. In an American history class, if you don't know the answer, respond with, "Grover Cleveland."

244. Know all five of the Great Lakes, west to east.

245. Know the name of your university's chancellor.

246. Make eye contact with professors and nod your head.

247. Write down anything a professor says that you didn't already know.

248. Own an extra pair of shoelaces.

249. Know that Nobel invented dynamite.

250. Always ask why if you question your grade.

251. Be respectful of professors and students.

252. Know the names of your high school prom dates, or at least pretend you know them. Once someone finds out you don't remember who you went to prom with, they may worry you place little importance on people.

253. Own an eraser and an extra pencil.

254. Never trust anyone with pointy fingers.

255. Don't date anyone you haven't known for at least two months.

256. Buy a calculator.

257. If it's all you can eat, eat lots of cheese.

258. Know where the nearest vending machine is, no matter where you are.

259. Never wear horizontal stripes.

260. Check out a locker at the campus rec.

261. Be outside every chance you get.

262. Don't snitch.

263. Never give out your Facebook or Myspace password. (This tip takes me way back.)

264. Don't go to bed angry.

265. Never go anywhere alone with someone you don't know well.

266. Never cheat.

267. Eat an apple or piece of fresh fruit every morning... It will get your metabolism going and freshen your breath. There's also nothing wrong with taking care of your body once in a while.

268. If professors allow you to email papers, also have a hard copy available. Not only is it good for personal reference, it's also way easier than having to try to find a printer and reliable internet connection.

269. Don't allow incriminating pictures to be put online.

270. Know where to find the nearest bathroom.

271. Chew gum constantly.

272. Shake hands firmly.

273. Don't wear clothes with stains on them.

274. Go to a concert once a month.

275. Comb or brush your hair before leaving your room.

276. Use mouthwash.

277. Don't litter on campus, or anywhere.

278. Invest in a permanent marker.

279. Carry dental floss in your backpack.

280. Always know what time it is.

281. Make sure your shoes fit.

282. Always know where you put your debit card.

283. Clean your mirror.

284. Don't put gum on your bedpost.

285. Invest in a reading light.

286. Keep everything you own on your side of the room.

287. Buy toenail clippers.

288. Rinse the bathroom sink after using it.

289. Always flush the toilet.

290. Brush your tongue.

291. Put lids on bottles very tightly.

292. Be the first to class on test days.

293. Make sure no one is looking off your test.

294. Show your parents your dorm room.

295. Buy your own soap
and shampoo.

296. Use lotion.

297. Don't walk around in socks, or
they'll get wet, and you don't
want to know with what.

298. Don't use extension cords.

299. Learn how to use chopsticks.

300. Drink chocolate milk every
chance you get.

301. Eat red meat at least once a
week. This keeps your iron
levels up; otherwise, you'll
be sleepy.

302. Don't buy friends
expensive gifts.

303. Use the same signature every time.

304. Be proud of your middle name.

305. Wash your shoes once a week.

306. Take a multivitamin.

307. Know the actors in your favorite movie.

308. Don't drink hot chocolate through a straw.

309. Never spit on campus. Not only is it gross, but some cultures around the world view this as extremely disrespectful.

310. Don't throw your gum on the sidewalk.

311. Have access to a flashlight.

312. Store the phone number of two cab companies.

313. Wipe your feet when entering any building.

314. Buy your own printer.

315. Don't rely on wireless internet.

316. Write down important dates.

317. Highlight in your text books.

318. Use folders.

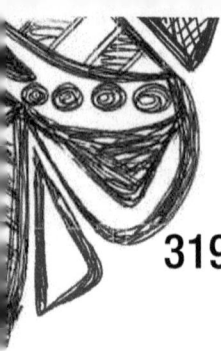

319. Have access to crayons. This one's simply for pleasure.

320. Go to a mall every two weeks.

321. Check your mail every day.

322. Clean your computer screen.

323. Don't drink water that isn't from a fountain or freshly opened bottle.

324. Never hit anyone—first or last.

325. Get your own bank account.

326. Use chapstick.

327. Carry tissues in your backpack.

328. Have extra batteries on hand.

329. Own at least one pair of flip flops.

330. Watch a Vietnam movie.

331. Be sure to reset your clocks during daylight savings time.

332. Drink tea.

333. Know the name of at least one Greek Titan.

334. Call your grandparents at least twice a month.

335. Be able to name two songs by Beethoven.

336. Go to a ballet once every five years.

337. Know where free activities in your city are.

338. Don't pay more than two dollars for a hot dog.

339. Watch your sodium intake.

340. No matter what you're doing, acknowledge whoever is speaking.

341. Know at least twenty-five movie quotations.

342. Know who sings your favorite song.

343. Go to a museum once a year.

344. Be able to identify your favorite painting.

345. Find your wallet or purse at least once an hour.

346. Own a can opener.

347. Try drinking iced coffee.

348. Eat ice cream once a week.

349. Find out your blood type.

350. Consider being an organ donor.

351. Eat outside on nice days.

352. Carpool whenever possible.

353. Have bookmarks in all your textbooks.

354. Don't burn bridges.

355. Don't own fish.

356. Hang up all your clothes.

357. Don't talk behind anyone's back.

358. Own an airplane pillow.

359. Elevate your feet at night after a long day.

360. Participate in canned food drives.

361. Try eating a new food once a month.

362. Don't abuse ginseng.

363. Keep in constant contact with siblings.

364. Tell your loved ones you love them.

365. Buy hoodies that have zippers.

366. Own a headband.

367. Try tanning at least once.

368. Be able to recognize George Washington.

369. Know when President's Day is.

370. Visit the physician on campus.

371. Go to the dentist in your hometown.

372. Never make fun of someone's religion.

373. Never make fun of someone's mother.

374. Remember the name of your favorite children's book.

375. Write a poem for your parents.

376. Always say please.

377. Always say thank you.

378. Don't get angry at people who drive slowly.

379. Don't be in a hurry, no matter what you're doing.

380. Take a health education class.

381. Refer to little people as little people, but use their name if you know it.

382. Clean the keys on your laptop.

383. Never call anyone fat.

384. Take time to watch your favorite TV show.

385. Get your oil changed on time.

386. Take ten minutes at the end of every day to reflect.

387. Don't take things more seriously than they are.

388. Keep duct tape nearby.

389. Don't get tricked into buying a fountain pen.

390. Dye your hair a weird color at least once.

391. Read the comics.

392. Know the rules to sports you play.

393. Carry a toothbrush everywhere you go.

394. Stockpile napkins.

395. Never let your gas tank get below a quarter full.

396. Get your tires rotated.

397. Go on road trips.

398. Never go to a college because of a boyfriend or girlfriend of less than three years.

399. Professors are way more understanding than you'd expect. Ask them anything.

400. You can prepare brownies in the microwave.

401. Never wear socks with sandals.

402. Don't brag about body noises.

403. Keep your glove compartment clean.

404. Use the restroom before class.

405. Rub your temples twice a day.

406. Don't use cotton swabs if you're in a hurry.

407. Take a yoga class.

408. Eat yogurt.

409. Brush the roof of your mouth when you brush your teeth.

410. Don't take no for an answer when turned down at a job interview.

411. Make yourself marketable.

412. Go to the movies once a month.

413. Know a book on the bestseller list.

414. Put pepper on french fries.

415. Eat the skin on your baked potato.

416. Get a cell phone plan with unlimited texting.

417. Purchase a digital camera.

418. Throw away clipped nails.

419. If it snows, leave at least fifteen minutes earlier than planned.

420. Don't run if it's raining.

421. Bring along your old portable CD player.

422. Don't spend more than seventy-five dollars on anything.

423. Tie trash bags before taking them out of the can.

424. Crush all boxes you are throwing away

425. Pretend you don't know what a MILF is.

426. Watch lots of game shows.

427. Don't take your debit card to a casino.

428. Know which person is on each American bill.

429. Never try to walk backwards in front of other people.

430. Put a piece of reflective tape on the back of your backpack.

431. Write your name on every piece of your laptop, including your power cord.

432. Own at least two long sleeved tee shirts.

433. Eat an ounce of nuts regularly.

434. Don't blow bubbles with your gum—ever.

435. Wash your hands whenever you think about it.

436. Don't play video games more than half an hour per day.

437. Do something alone at least once a week.

438. Learn how to use the phone in your dorm room.

439. After leaving the restroom, check your front and back in the mirror.

440. Organize the drawers in your desk.

441. Make your laundry last as long as possible.

442. Buy a clothes hamper.

443. Enjoy downtime.

444. Always wear pants with pockets.

445. Keep a broom in your dorm room.

446. Try swimming for exercise.

447. Keep a folder with all your syllabi.

448. Know your way around the library.

449. Don't drag your feet when walking.

450. Try paintballing.

451. Try frolf (frisbee golf).

452. Go to a symphony.

453. Never leave your food unattended at a table.

454. Don't eat more than one serving of junk food at a given time.

Add your own tip or artwork.

ACKNOWLEDGMENTS

A special thanks and much love to the people who helped throughout this whole process, my family, especially my parents, my siblings, and my daughter. Thanks to Michele for the support and awesome artwork. A shout out to all the people who were with me through these unforgettable stories, questionable decisions, and life altering moments, especially Will, Kalen, Jon, Matt, DJ, and Jason. Thanks to Kelli for her patience and always allowing me to vent; Sarah for help in editing; Lisa, Rachel, and Ellie for helping bring this to life.

Add your own tip or artwork.

STRESS RELIEF

Since you're early for class and eager for the next exhilarating lecture, this section is here to provide stress relief, as well as improve your coloring skills.

I make new

FRIENDS

ABOUT THE AUTHOR

Stattin Yates was born and raised in Bellevue, Nebraska. He graduated from the University of Nebraska at Omaha with his degree in Secondary Education, Social Sciences and was on the chancellor's list. He was active around campus and never turned down a chance to be around friends, meet new people, and attend a concert or a hockey game. After graduating, Yates traveled around the US for a year and then took a job teaching Psychology, Sociology, and Law in Omaha Public Schools. He was inspired to write this book because after five years of teaching high school seniors, he saw a potential to help them fill the gap between high school and college with his college experience. Now, Yates lives in Omaha, Nebraska, and focuses on writing and other business ventures.